Assessing Post-fire Douglas-fir Mortality and Douglas-fir Beetle Attacks in the Northern Rocky Mountains

Supplement

United States Department of Agriculture / Forest Service

Rocky Mountain Research Station

General Technical Report RMRS-GTR-199 Supplement

September 2007

Hood, Sharon; Bentz, Barbara; Gibson, Ken; Ryan, Kevin; DeNitto, Gregg. 2007. **Assessing post-fire Douglas-fir mortality and Douglas-fir beetle attacks in the northern Rocky Mountains.** Gen. Tech. Rep. RMRS-GTR-199 Supplement. Fort Collins, CO: U.S. Department of Agriculture, Forest Service, Rocky Mountain Research Station. 18 p.

Abstract

Douglas-fir have life history traits that greatly enhance resistance to injury from fire, thereby increasing post-fire survival rates. Tools for predicting the probability of tree mortality following fire are important components of both pre-fire planning and post-fire management. Hood and Bentz (2007) developed models for predicting the probability of Douglas-fir mortality and Douglas-fir bark beetle attack in the Northern Rocky Mountains based on fire injury and stand characteristics. This supplemental field guide to RMRS-GTR-199 provides reference photographs to help quantify injury level for use with the post-fire Douglas-fir mortality and bark beetle attack models. It also includes descriptions for measuring each characteristic in the field.

Upper left photo: Kevin Halverson estimates crown volume scorched.
Lower left photo: Jackie Redmer checks for cambium injury.

You may order additional copies of this publication by sending your mailing information in label form through one of the following media. Please specify the publication title and series number.

Fort Collins Service Center

Telephone	(970) 498-1392
FAX	(970) 498-1122
E-mail	rschneider@fs.fed.us
Web site	http://www.fs.fed.us/rm/publications
Mailing address	Publications Distribution
	Rocky Mountain Research Station
	240 West Prospect Road
	Fort Collins, CO 80526

Rocky Mountain Research Station
Natural Resources Research Center
2150 Centre Blvd., Building A
Fort Collins, CO 80526

Authors

Sharon Hood is a Forester with the Rocky Mountain Research Station at the Fire Sciences Laboratory in Missoula, Montana. She completed a B.S. in Forestry from Mississippi State University and a M.S. in Forestry from Virginia Polytechnic Institute and State University.

Barbara Bentz is a Research Entomologist with the Rocky Mountain Research Station located in Logan, UT. She received Forestry degrees from Stephen F. Austin State University and the University of Idaho, and a Ph.D. in Entomology from Virginia Polytechnic Institute and State University.

Ken Gibson is an Entomologist, USDA Forest Service, Forest Health Protection, Missoula, MT. He completed a B.S. in Forest Management and M.S. in Forest Entomology from the University of Missouri.

Kevin Ryan is currently the Program Manager for the LANDFIRE National Landscape Fire Management Planning Tools Project at the Missoula Fire Sciences Laboratory. He completed a B.S. in Forest Biology and a M.S. in Fire Ecology from Colorado State University, and a Ph.D. in Forest Ecology from the University of Montana.

Gregg DeNitto is the Group Leader of the Missoula field office of Forest Health Protection in the Northern Region of the USDA Forest Service in Missoula, MT. He completed a B.A. degree in Biology/Forestry at Thiel College and a Ph.D. in Forest Pathology at Duke University.

Acknowledgments

This project was funded in part by the Forest Service, U.S. Department of Agriculture, Forest Health Protection Region 1, the Beaverhead-Deerlodge National Forest (agreement number 0102-01-010), the Special Technology Development Program (R4-2004-02), and the Joint Fire Science Program (05-2-1-105). We thank Chris Fettig, Kjerstin Skov and Heidi Trechsel for helpful comments on an earlier draft of this manuscript.

Contents

Introduction

This field guide is to be used in conjunction with the accompanying RMRS-GTR-199. Included are photographs depicting a range of fire-related injuries for Douglas-fir and associated descriptions and instructions for quantifying injury level in the field. The guide is intended for use with Douglas-fir greater than 5 inches in DBH. The characteristics included were found to be most significant in predicting post-fire Douglas-fir tree mortality and Douglas-fir bark beetle attack, and are used in models developed by Hood and Bentz (2007) and described in accompanying RMRS-GTR-199.

Percent Crown Volume Scorched

Percent crown volume scorched is assessed by visually estimating percent of pre-fire crown volume that was killed by fire. Scorched and blackened needles will soon drop from the crown. Therefore, crown scorch should be evaluated within 1 year post-fire. Figures 1 through 9 show a range of crown scorch. To evaluate crown scorch:

- First, position yourself in such a way that the entire tree crown is visible. Optimum viewing of the crown is at right angles to the direction of the fire spread and against a blue sky. It is important to stand back from the tree to fully view the entire crown.

- Next, reconstruct what the crown looked like before the fire. A tree with no bark and charred wood was dead before the fire. Pre-fire crown volume can be estimated by looking at the fine branch structure and needles. Branches lacking fine twigs were likely dead before the fire.

- Next, look at the overall appearance of the crown and estimate the percent of crown volume killed by fire based on your estimated pre-fire crown area. This includes any areas with brown, "frozen" needles, as well as any areas that have blackened fine branches. Blackened twigs may have some blackened needles remaining.

- Keep in mind overall crown shape. If, for example, the tree is cone shaped, 50 percent crown scorch may not equal 50 percent of the pre-fire crown length. Also, be sure to look at all sides of the tree. It is possible to have very high crown scorch on one side, but low crown scorch on the opposite side.

Cambium Kill Rating (CKR)

Cambium Kill Rating (CKR) is the number of dead cambium samples based on four samples per tree (fig. 10). The cambium, or phloem, is the living portion of the tree bole found between the bark and the wood (fig 11). To determine CKR:

- Nick bark away at ground-line using a hatchet on one side of the tree to expose the cambium (fig. 12). As small an area of bark as possible should be removed to prevent further injury to the tree. It is important to sample as close to the ground-line as possible, as this is where injury to the cambium from heat is most likely to occur. Douglas-fir has thick, light and dark colored bark, so be careful to bore completely through the bark to see this cambium layer.

- Once cambium is exposed, determine if it is live or dead.

  - Live tissue will feel moist, soft, and spongy, and will be a light pink, salmon color (fig. 13). Live cambium is pliable and usually, is easily peeled away from the wood and bark.

  - Dead cambium either will be hardened, with a dark, shiny appearance (fig. 14) or will feel sticky, with a darker color, and a sour smell (fig. 15). Sometimes the resin may have dried and have a whitish cast (fig. 16, lower area). Dead cambium will not easily separate from the wood and bark.

- Sometimes the sample will contain both live and dead cambium (fig. 16). In this situation, count the sample as live cambium.

- Continue sampling cambium in this way on four, evenly spaced areas of the tree and sum the dead cambium samples. CKR for the tree is the number of dead samples (for example, 0 to 4).

Table 1. Bark char codes and description of bark appearance (adapted from Ryan 1982).

Bark char code	Bark appearance
Unburned	Not burned
Light	Evidence of light scorching; can still identify species based on bark characteristics; bark is not completely blackened; edges of bark plates charred
Moderate	Bark is uniformly black except possibly some inner fissures; bark characteristics still discernable
Deep	Bark has been burned into, but not necessarily to the wood; outer characteristics are lost

To speed sampling time, bark char codes can be used instead of direct sampling of cambium (table 1, fig. 17), although doing so will reduce accuracy (fig. 1, GTR-199). When using bark char codes:

- Divide the tree bole into 4 quadrants (fig. 10).

- Assess each quadrant at ground-line to determine the bark char code. Bark char is often lighter higher on the bole than at ground-line, but only the area at ground-line should be considered. If the fire was low intensity and only the duff and litter burned, there may only be charring very low on the bole (fig. 18).

- Cambium beneath bark on a quadrant with unburned or light char can be assumed to be alive.

- Cambium beneath deep bark char can be assumed dead. Deep bark char is generally found only where an object near the tree base, such as a fallen tree, stump, or deep duff, burned for a long period of time.

- Direct sampling of cambium should be conducted if bark char is moderate because moderate bark char does not accurately predict if underlying cambium is live or dead.

Douglas-fir Beetle Attack-Level

Douglas-fir beetle adults are 0.16 to 0.24 inches long with a black body and reddish-brown wing covers (fig. 19). Douglas-fir beetles require live phloem for successful brood production and survival. Beetles also tend to attack trees growing in denser areas, with DBH greater than 9 inches. Attacked trees are identified based on external bole signs such as reddish-orange boring dust (fig. 18), a result of adult beetles chewing through bark into the inner cambium. Other insects may be found attacking fire-injured Douglas-fir. In particular, wood borers in the families Cerambycidae and Buprestidae produce a fine white granular boring dust rather than the reddish-orange dust produced by Douglas-fir beetle. Other insects only attack near the base of the tree, whereas Douglas-fir beetle attacks occur continuously along the height of the tree bole.

To assess Douglas-fir beetle attack status from ground-level:

- Look up the tree bole as high as possible for signs of boring. Initial attacks by Douglas-fir beetle typically occur high (~12 ft.) on tree boles with additional attacks above and below that height. The entire circumference of the bole should be examined, noting percent of bole circumference with signs of reddish-orange boring dust. Boring dust may be found between crevices on the bark and/or on the ground surrounding the bole of attacked trees.

- Clear resin flow or 'streamers' on the upper portion of a tree bole may be a sign of Douglas-fir beetle attack, but is often merely a tree response to fire injury. Therefore streamers are not a reliable indicator of beetle attack (fig. 20).

- To confirm presence of Douglas-fir beetle, a small portion of bark can be removed to reveal parent and larval galleries in the inner cambium (fig. 21).

- We estimate that trees with signs of boring dust on 10 percent to 90 percent of the bole circumference are strip-attacked and trees with greater than 90 percent of the bole circumference with boring signs are mass-attacked. Mass-attacked trees will die regardless of fire injury.

- When tallying data for the tree mortality model, all trees strip- and mass-attacked (greater than 10 percent of bole circumference with signs of boring) should be recorded as attacked. If boring dust is found on less than 10 percent of the tree bole, the tree is recorded as unattacked.

References

Hood, S. M.; Bentz, B. 2007. Predicting post-fire Douglas-fir beetle attacks and tree mortality in the Northern Rocky Mountains. Canadian Journal of Forest Research. 37: 1058-1069.

Ryan, K. C. 1982. Techniques for assessing fire damage to trees. In: Lotan, J., ed. Proceedings of the symposium: Fire, its field effects; 1982 October 19-21; Jackson, Wyoming. Missoula, MT: Intermountain Fire Council: 1-11.

Figure 1. Douglas-fir with 10 percent crown volume scorched. Only the lowermost branches and tips of some of the upper branches are scorched.

Figure 2. Douglas-fir with 20 percent crown volume scorched. The scorch on this tree is higher on one side than the other, as shown by the diagonal line delineating the uppermost scorch. This pattern of crown scorch is often seen in steep areas.

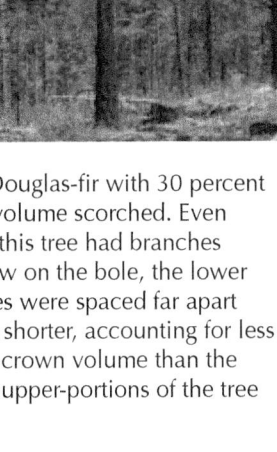

Figure 3. Douglas-fir with 30 percent crown volume scorched. Even though this tree had branches fairly low on the bole, the lower branches were spaced far apart and are shorter, accounting for less pre-fire crown volume than the mid- to upper-portions of the tree crown.

Figure 4. Douglas-fir with 40 percent crown volume scorched. Crown scorch is most accurately assessed by standing far enough back to view the whole crown. If the area is on a steep slope, move uphill or to the side of the tree in question, as done in this picture, to frame the crown against a blue sky.

Figure 5. Douglas-fir with 50 percent crown volume scorched. A) The short, lower branches of this tree were dead before the fire and should not be included when determining crown scorch. Branches that were dead before the fire will not have any fine twigs and will often be broken off. B) Trees often have unsymmetrical crown bases as seen here. It may help to "move" some of the lower branches to the other side of the crown to even out the crown bases and then estimate crown scorch based on this new crown shape.

Figure 6. Douglas-fir with 60 percent crown volume scorched. A) Be careful to look at all sides of the tree–the crown scorch is much lower on the back side of this tree. B) A tree with high scorch on all sides of the crown. The lower, short branches were dead before the fire. Be careful to include only the branches that have fine twigs when estimating pre-fire crown volume.

Pre-fire crown base

Figure 8. Douglas-fir with 90 percent crown volume scorched. Very few green needles remain in the crown with this high level of crown scorch.

Figure 7. Douglas-fir with 80 percent crown volume scorched.

Figure 9. Douglas-fir with 100 percent crown volume scorched. Green needles are absent in the crown.

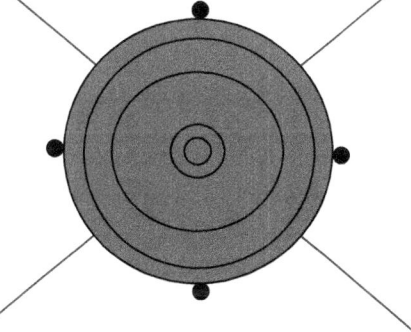

Figure 10. Cross-section of tree showing placement of cambium samples to determine cambium kill rating (CKR). Black circles represent placement of direct cambium samples. Cambium should be sampled as close to the ground-line as possible. The lines show how to divide the tree bole into four bark char quadrants when using bark char codes in place of direct cambium sampling.

Figure 11. Cross-section of Douglas-fir showing cambium layer between bark and wood. In this photo, the cambium is seen as a dark band because it is dead.

Figure 12. Use a hatchet to expose a small section of cambium at ground-line to determine cambium status. The cambium seen here is live. Douglas-fir bark has both light and dark sections. Be careful to chop completely through the bark to expose the cambium.

Figure 13. Live Douglas-fir cambium is salmon colored, moist, spongy, and pliable.

Figure 14. Dead Douglas-fir cambium. The cambium here has dried up to a very thin layer that cannot be separated from the wood beneath it.

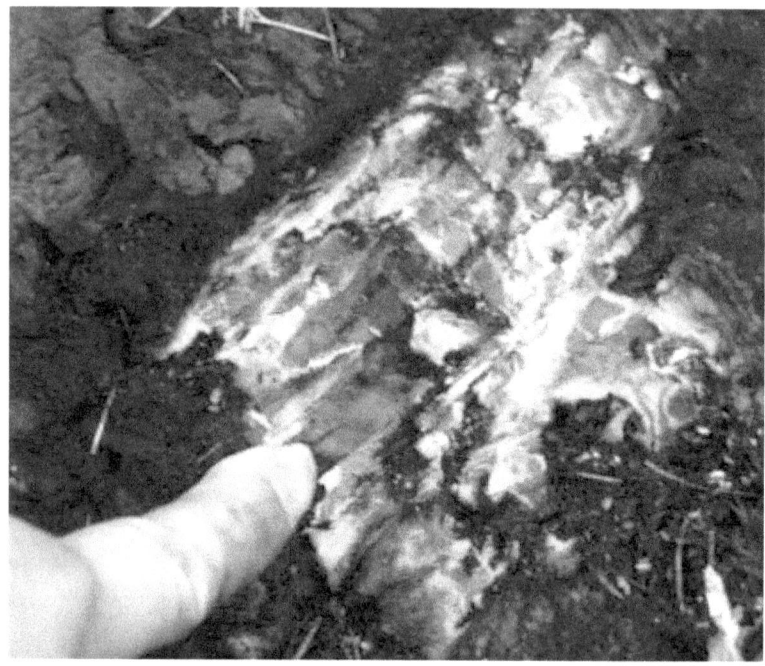

Figure 15. Dead Douglas-fir cambium is darker in color. It may have a sour smell and be moist; however, it will feel sticky and is not spongy.

Figure 16. Boundary between live and dead Douglas-fir cambium. The dead cambium here has a whitish cast because of the dried resin. If both live and dead cambium are found in one sample, count the sample as live for purposes of determining cambium kill rating (CKR).

Figure 17. Bark char on Douglas-fir. A) unburned bark, B) light bark char, C) moderate bark char, D) deep bark char. See table 1 for a description of each bark char code.

Figure 18. Sharp transition between unburned and moderate bark char. The bark char is very low on the tree due to low intensity fire burning only the duff and litter around the tree. When using bark char codes, always examine the area of bark nearest the ground-line to determine the correct code. The orange piles of boring dust on the bole are from Douglas-fir beetle attacks.

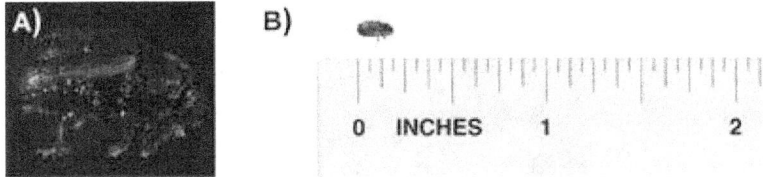

Figure 19. A) Enlarged picture of Douglas-fir beetle to show detail. B) Life-sized Douglas-fir beetle.

Figure 20. Streamers of pitch are not a reliable indicator that the tree is attacked by Douglas-fir beetle.

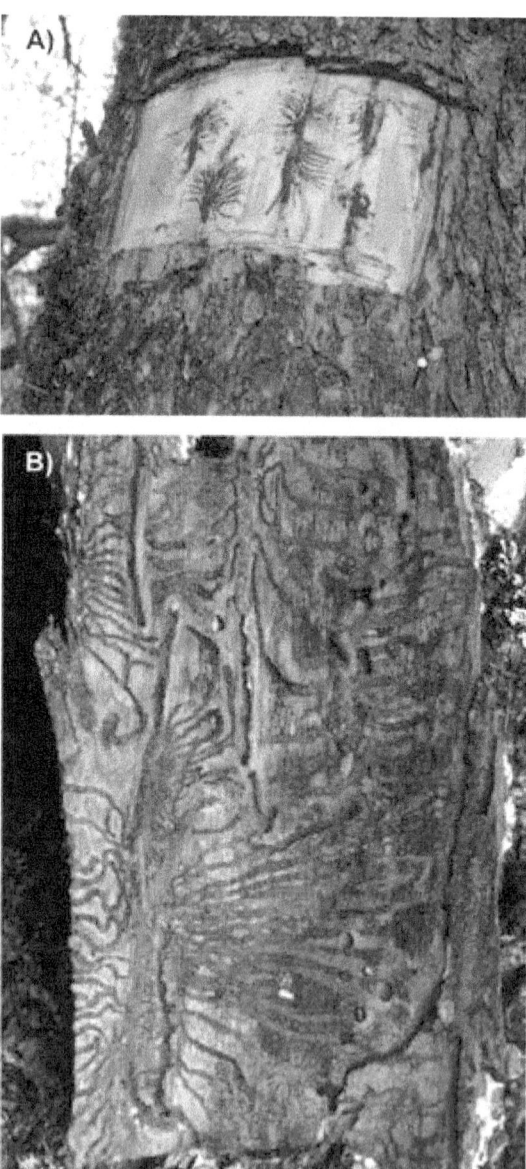

Figure 21. Douglas-fir beetle galleries. Each bark beetle species constructs a unique gallery pattern. A) The Douglas-fir beetle galleries here are within weeks of attack and are not fully developed. B) Fully developed Douglas-fir beetle galleries.

RMRS
ROCKY MOUNTAIN RESEARCH STATION

The Rocky Mountain Research Station develops scientific information and technology to improve management, protection, and use of the forests and rangelands. Research is designed to meet the needs of the National Forest managers, Federal and State agencies, public and private organizations, academic institutions, industry, and individuals.
Studies accelerate solutions to problems involving ecosystems, range, forests, water, recreation, fire, resource inventory, land reclamation, community sustainability, forest engineering technology, multiple use economics, wildlife and fish habitat, and forest insects and diseases. Studies are conducted cooperatively, and applications may be found worldwide.

Research Locations

Flagstaff, Arizona	Reno, Nevada
Fort Collins, Colorado*	Albuquerque, New Mexico
Boise, Idaho	Rapid City, South Dakota
Moscow, Idaho	Logan, Utah
Bozeman, Montana	Ogden, Utah
Missoula, Montana	Provo, Utah

*Station Headquarters, Natural Resources Research Center, 2150 Centre Avenue, Building A, Fort Collins, CO 80526.

www.ingramcontent.com/pod-product-compliance
Lightning Source LLC
Chambersburg PA
CBHW060022300526
45794CB00003B/1261